ACTION REPLAY!
Flick here to see
the wagons roll!

Contents

Other titles in the *Speedy Reads* series:

Moon Landing by Nick Arnold
Titanic by Alan MacDonald
The True Mystery of the Mary Celeste
by Rachel Wright

GOLD
RUSH

Valerie Wilding
Illustrated by Pete Smith

■SCHOLASTIC

Scholastic Children's Books
Commonwealth House, 1-19 New Oxford Street
London WC1A 1NU, UK

A division of Scholastic Ltd
London ~ New York ~ Toronto ~ Sydney ~ Auckland
Mexico City ~ New Delhi ~ Hong Kong

First published in the UK by Scholastic Ltd, 2001

ISBN: 0 439 99951 0

Typeset by Falcon Oast Graphic Art Ltd.
Printed by Cox & Wyman Ltd, Reading, Berks.

2 4 6 8 10 9 7 5 3 1

Gold rush!

America, 1849

The steady rumble of wooden wheels never stops, as wagon after wagon rushes across the continent. Thousands of men, some with wives and children, are heading west to California on a dangerous and uncomfortable journey into the unknown. Others, choosing different routes, brave storms at sea, or hack through snake-infested jungle. They all have the same goal, and no amount of hardships will put them off. Not everyone will make it. But for those who do – dreams could come true.

And all because, on January 24, 1848, a man called James Marshall made a discovery which would change the face of America – for ever.

What's Marshall got to do with wagon trains?

To find out, let's slip back a year, to 1847. Queen Victoria was on the British throne, and Charles Dickens, after a whirlwind tour of America was almost as famous there as he was at home. American gunsmith Samuel Colt was making a bomb through his invention, the revolver and before the Gold Rush was over, sewing machines, crisps and frankfurters would make their appearance for the first time.

And what about California?
Well, forget Hollywood, surfing and all that "California Dreaming" stuff. In 1847, California was just plain sleepy. On the coast, the small port of San Francisco, with its population of under a thousand, basked in sunshine.

Who lived there?
No film stars yet. Instead there was a mixture of Mexicans, Native Americans, settlers from other parts of North America, and a sprinkling of Europeans. There were less than 20,000 settlers in California – hardly enough to raise a good cheer at a Cup Final. They were mainly farmers and cattle ranchers. There wasn't much else to do.

And where was the rest of the great American nation?

Back east, that's where. And they were happy to stay there. Great cities like New York were busy, lively, happenin' places. Who'd want to spend six months crossing the continent on a dangerous journey that would take you away from your warm bed, your mates and all those home comforts?

No, those farmers could keep their wide open spaces.

So California was owned by a load of farmers?

Well, not really – the land belonged to Mexico, the country to the south of California. America was at

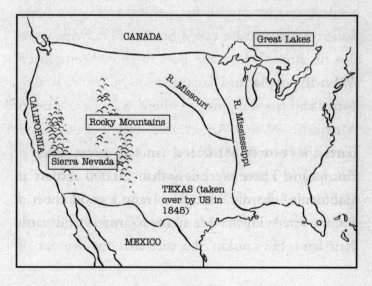

war with Mexico over who got to keep the state of Texas. California's future depended on the result of this Mexican War. If the Americans won, they would demand that the Mexicans hand over land – lots of land. And California would be part of the deal. Most of the people working the land probably weren't too bothered who came out on top – but one man was. Captain John Sutter was rather uneasy.

What's he got to do with it?

John Sutter was a Swiss shopkeeper who'd settled in California's flat Sacramento Valley. He was a bit of a tycoon, running lots of money-spinning businesses. He supplied the locals with just about anything they needed, and he ran all his businesses from a huge walled settlement he called Sutter's Fort, which was also his home. He made pots of money, employed loads of people and kept masses of cattle, mules, horses and hogs!

Doesn't your heart bleed for the poor man?

OK, he had a nice life, but Sutter worried about the outcome of the war. He had a lot to lose. Sutter had done a deal with the Mexicans to build his fort on their land. He couldn't be sure that the winner of the war would allow him to keep his lands . . . and his very nice lifestyle. He had to start something new, somewhere else – something that could make him even more money – just in case.

Was there anything he hadn't already thought of?

Not a lot, but Sutter spotted a gap in the market. One thing that even he was short of was good timber for building. So he decided to build a sawmill somewhere where the right timber was plentiful. Then he'd have all the wood he needed, and could sell the rest to anyone who needed timber for building – and that meant just about everyone.

In August, 1847, he went into partnership with a man called James Marshall.

So what did Marshall have to offer?

Sutter was a businessman – the money man behind the idea – but he needed someone who knew about timber. Marshall was a carpenter who could turn his hand to all sorts of things, and he had a lot of experience with mills.

He found the perfect site for his sawmill at Coloma, in the Sierra Nevada, on the American

River. There were plenty of pine trees, and the logs could be floated 50 miles downriver to Sutter's Fort. Cheap transport!

Marshall and his men set to work, first building log cabins for themselves to live in. Then they started on the sawmill, and damming the river.

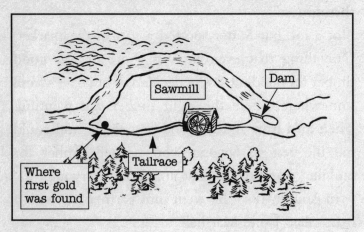

Who said dam it?

Marshall did! Water that built up behind the dam flowed down a new channel that ran through the mill and powered the big mill wheel. This new channel was called the millrace.

The end of the channel that carried water back to the river was called the tailrace. But water was flowing backwards through the tailrace and slowing the wheel. The channel had to be deepened.

Did they dig the idea?

No, they didn't – digging was too much like hard work. Marshall let the river do the work. He allowed fast-running water to rush through the channel all night. It made the channel deeper, washing sand and gravel into the main river, and something else besides. . .

Silence is . . . golden

24th January, 1848.
James Marshall wanders along beside the mill stream. He
spots something glinting in the shallow water. He picks it
up. Another gleam catches his eye . . . and another. . .
  Suspicion grows.
  Marshall's heart begins to thud.
  Gold! Gold!

Does he flip his lid?

Not quite! He stares down at his handful of
gleaming pebbles. It can't be gold, he reasons. It'll be
fool's gold – iron pyrite. People who don't know any
better mistake that yellow crystalline mineral for real
gold. Still . . . there's one way to find out. Fool's gold
is brittle. It can be crushed and shattered.

Marshall takes a large stone and raises it above his
head.

Smash!

He bashes the golden pebble. Again and again he brings the stone down. Smash! Smash! Smash!

Is it gold?

Well, the pebble hasn't shattered. He's beaten it flat. It's not brittle – it's soft. But surely it should be brighter than this? Marshall decides that his gold must be mixed with some other metal.

Does he get digging?

No, he hurries back for breakfast. The cook, Mrs Wimmer, gets stroppy if her food's kept waiting. Over breakfast, he shows his find to Peter Wimmer, Henry Bigler and the few other men he works most closely with. "Boys," he says, "I believe I have found a gold mine!"

Bet that makes them sit up?

Yes and no. Like Marshall, they're not too sure at first.

"Let's boil it in lye," one suggests. Lye, mixed with baking soda, is a *very* strong washing solution – you wouldn't want to dunk your best T-shirt in that mixture. They boil up a golden pebble in a cooking pot. When they take it out, the colour hasn't changed, and if there's one thing they know about pure gold, it's that it doesn't change.

FAST FACTS

Gold isn't affected by air or water. It won't go rusty, which means that gold items can stay buried for thousands of years without deteriorating.

So they shout "Gold!" from the hilltops?
Not likely. Marshall and his men want to collect any more gold that might be lying around for themselves. So, from then on, it's eyes open and mouths shut. They don't want to share their find. Over the next few days, they pick up several more pieces, each time thinking it might be the last of their haul.

But there's more?
Lots! Every night more gold is washed into the millrace, and soon Marshall decides he'd better tell Captain Sutter about their find. After all, they're partners, and Sutter can help make more tests. They still don't know for sure that it truly is gold. Marshall swears all the men to secrecy. On January 28, 1848, he saddles up and rides to Sutter's Fort.

14

Well, *is* it gold?

Marshall arrives rain-soaked. Dripping all over Sutter's floor, he demands weighing scales and a basin of water. "Lock the door," he tells Sutter.

They're alone. Only now does Marshall unroll the cloth containing his precious possession.

Once Sutter has the full story he, too, knows they must make absolutely sure the gold is genuine. He looks up "gold" in his encyclopaedia, and finds out how to test it.

How does it score?

Test	Result	
1 They bash it, to prove it's soft not brittle.	It can be hammered till it's thin.	Good news.
2 They weigh it against some silver coins to see if it's heavier.	It is heavier.	Great!
3 They put the scales in water. Is their metal denser than the silver?	The "gold" side sinks quickly.	Yesss!!

15

Test	Result	
4 They test their metal with aqua fortis★.	The gold is unchanged.	Yeeee-*hah*!!!

So it is gold?

It's gold. It's practically the purest gold. Sutter and Marshall know they must keep it to themselves, or the place will be heaving with strangers before they can say "rich pickin's". So it's back to the sawmill. They warn the men that if they talk, the whole area will be overrun with gold prospectors wielding pick-axes, and they'll all lose out. The men agree. After all, they can stroll down to the millrace any old time and, using just a pocket-knife, pick up a few flakes of gold as easily as picking a chocolate chip out of a fresh-baked cookie.

However, there's a small nagging doubt in Sutter's brain. The land his sawmill is built on is public land. Nobody really owns it. Hmm. . .

★Aqua fortis means "strong water" and is another name for nitric acid. It dissolves out anything that isn't gold, but leaves real gold unharmed.

Does he grab it for himself?

He tries. Sutter figures that the only people with any true rights to the land are the local Native Americans, the Coloma Valley Indians, so he does a quick deal with them. He swaps a couple of hundred dollars worth of clothes, food and other goods from his store for the use of the land around the mill. Crafty!

Safe at last?

Sutter soon has a nasty shock. The Mexican war is over, and the end-of-war treaty, signed just nine days after Marshall discovered gold, means California is now firmly in the hands of the winner – America.

When Sutter tries to tie up his ownership and make it nice and legal, the local military governor, Colonel Mason, won't have it. The US has won the war, so the Native Americans – the local Indians – have no rights to the land, he says. Therefore, they had no right to hand it over to Sutter. He can't have it, whatever swap they've agreed. The land the sawmill stands on belongs to the United States Government.

Will the mill – and the gold – go up the creek?

No, Sutter has as much right as anyone else to be on that land. Unfortunately for him, so does the rest of the American population. His only hope now of keeping the gold for himself is to keep his mouth shut. After all, the only other people in on the secret are James Marshall, Peter Wimmer, Henry Bigler and a few other men.

Oh, and Mrs Wimmer, the cook. . .

Can they keep a secret?

No chance! It seeps out in several ways. Mrs Wimmer tells Jacob Wittmer, one of Sutter's delivery men. Wittmer gathers a little gold for himself and takes the news back to Sutter's Fort. Henry Bigler mentions it when he writes to some friends working not far away. Even John Sutter is daft enough to boast about his find in a letter.

Is everybody happy?

You bet your life they are. Sutter's men do a little gold-hunting of their own. After all, the gold is almost on the surface. All they need is a knife. But soon, a few nuggets a day aren't enough for Henry Bigler. He has bigger ideas. He's caught gold fever, and heads off to start prospecting for himself.

Gold fever is starting to spread like chicken pox.

A cunning plan!

Within a few weeks, all Sutter's men made big career changes and deserted him. His labourers, cooks, clerks – all his employees at the Fort – switched to the same profession. Gold prospecting. There were golden opportunities for all!

So had the rush officially started?
Strangely, the rest of the world didn't seem fussed just yet. Gold fever certainly affected most of the locals but, even though rumours of a gold strike spread as far as San Francisco on the coast, nobody there took much notice.

Except a man called Sam Brannan.

Who's Sam Brannan when he's at home?
Brannan started San Francisco's first newspaper and he dabbled in all sorts of deals. He was sharp, and

realized that California was a land of opportunities – opportunities to make a fortune.

Sam had a store inside the walls of Sutter's Fort. One of Sutter's men came to splash out on a bottle of brandy. His name was Jacob Wittmer – the very same Jacob Wittmer who'd heard a secret about a gold strike from Mrs Wimmer. Jacob paid for his brandy with gold.

When Sam Brannan heard about that, he was very, very interested.

So Sam went for gold?
Not exactly. Sam saw an easier way of making money. He opened a store right next to the sawmill, and stocked up with everything he could lay his hands on that might be useful to a gold miner. He made sure that Brannan's was the only place where a prospector could get what he needed to start mining, and Sam reckoned he knew just how to get those prospectors a-comin'.

What was his brilliant idea?
Simple. In May, 1848, he filled a medicine bottle with gold dust, and charged through the streets of San Francisco bellowing, "Gold! Gold! Gold from the American River!"

Surely they'd all heard that one before?
You're right. Rumours about gold strikes were as common as sailors in the dockside saloon bar, but most people knew from experience that they were just rumours.

But this time it was different.

They believed it?
You bet the San Franciscans believed it! Sam had the proof right there in his hand! And sleepy old California would never be the same again.

Was Sam chuffed with the result?
Tickled pink, was more like it! Sam Brannan expected hordes of people to head for the gold diggings, but even he couldn't have imagined the staggering effect of his parade through the port of San Francisco.

How long before the rush started?
About five minutes. People dropped what they were doing, locked up their shops and houses and headed for the American River, Sutter's Mill and a fortune (they hoped). Married men kissed their wives goodbye. Soldiers left their posts, and whole crews

deserted their ships. School closed due to lack of teachers, and notices appeared on shop doors, saying simply: "Gone to the diggings."

Brannan's rival newspaper, the *Californian,* trumpeted: "The whole country resounds with the sordid cry of gold! GOLD! GOLD!" and reported that fields were left half-planted and houses half-built, and the manufacture of everything was neglected – except for shovels and pickaxes. But there was hardly anybody left to read the paper, or even print it, so soon it closed down too.

San Francisco lay almost deserted.

FAST FACTS
Within three weeks, the population of San Francisco shrank from about 812 to a couple of dozen.

Did the news stop in California?
Almost. Talk of gold spread locally, and towns like San José and Los Angeles suffered a similar fate to San Francisco.

But most of the American population still lived way over in the east (with hardly anybody in the middle), so once the news reached the outskirts of western settlements, it came to a halt. Ships normally carried news and rumours around the world, but the sailors were busy digging.

Didn't anybody in authority poke their nose in?

Oh, yes! Californian Governor Mason realized that the major gold strike everyone was talking about was on land belonging to the United States. He wondered about getting some sort of fee or land rent from the prospectors – for the government, of course – and visited the diggings. Once he'd looked around, he started writing a detailed report to the government.

Did Mason put the brakes on all that gold-gathering?

Not him! The thing was, he didn't really fancy the idea of going up to hundreds of rough, tough, grizzled gold prospectors and asking them for money. So Governor Mason decided to let things lie, and in August 1848, three months after Brannan first brandished his gold dust, he completed his report.

Did the government spill the beans?

The general public didn't get to hear about the report straight away, but there was a letter about it in the *New York Herald*.

Did New York go wild?

Wild? No. Not yet. It took a message to Congress (the American parliament) from the President himself – and a tea-caddy – finally to persuade them that the stories were true.

What's a tea-caddy got do with it?

Everything. Governor Mason had sent the tea-caddy to the President, along with his report. It contained six and a half kilograms of gold. If that didn't convince Congress, nothing would.

That must have made them sit up?

You bet! The gold was put on display for the rest of New York to see. *Then* they went wild!

The truth about the gold strike spread outwards from New York across the States. The whole nation was electrified. The news boarded ships and travelled the world. It was December, and the new year, 1849, was just around the corner.

'49 was to be a year America would never forget.

Off to see the elephant

Dire warnings of the danger, even madness, of travelling to the California diggings made little difference to excited prospectors. Gold fever was catching, and it seemed there was no cure.

Some prepared sensibly. Others simply dropped what they were doing and headed west. But easterners faced a long, perilous journey if they wanted to see the elephant.

But there aren't any elephants in America!
That's right! But travellers to California often said they were off "to see the elephant". It was a way of saying, "I'm headin' for a wild time, an' I'm gonna see things I ain't never seen before."

Who got there first?
Apart from the locals, the first prospectors to arrive

at the Californian diggings were Mexicans and those who happened to sail into San Francisco at the right time. They got the "easy pickings" – gold that was lying on the surface waiting to be picked out with the flick of a knife.

What about all those easterners?
They got there as fast as they could! Americans came by land or sea from the eastern side of the continent. African Americans came too, many as slaves owned by citizens of the Southern United States where slavery was still allowed. Some would put in a day's toil for their owners and then, instead of resting, they prospected for themselves. Quite a number worked so hard they gathered enough gold dust to buy their freedom.

Didn't foreigners want a piece of the action?
A big piece! As news spread, prospectors from all over the world set out for America, chasing their dreams. Thousands of Chinese came to *Gum San* – the Golden Mountain.

And did they all rub along nicely together?

Not necessarily. Many Americans thought the gold should be theirs alone, and resented foreigners muscling in on it. Sadly, many thought the Chinese were the lowest of the low. Americans simply refused to work alongside them. The hard-working Chinese were often driven off when they tried to stake their claims.

Did they take themselves away?

No, they used their loaves and found other ways of making money. Some took over abandoned gold diggings, and worked hard to sift what gold had been left there. Others ended up rolling in money without digging up a single speck of gold. They opened restaurants and laundries, giving excellent service – at a price.

So the gold rush affected people all over the world?

That's right. From wherever the news reached – places as far apart as Europe, Australia, Japan and Hawaii – brave, hopeful people struck out to make a better life for themselves. They included the needy *and* the greedy.

Crocs and cholera

In those days, travelling was nothing like the simple matter it is today. Journeys took time, and a lot of preparation. And they meant taking risks, especially when travelling through unknown territory. Let's take a look at some of the hazards the Argonauts faced.

Excuse me? Argonauts?

Ever heard the Greek myth about Jason, who searched for a Golden Fleece? His ship was called the *Argo*, and the men who sailed with him were known as Argonauts. The name came to mean anyone on a quest – especially a quest for gold.

Sounds like fun?

Oh, yes? Let's see how you'd make out as an Argonaut. You'd have a choice of three main routes to California from the east coast of America, which is where the first wave of Argonauts came from.

Any chance of a Californian cruise?

Actually, you *could* sail there. Here's how you'd travel by sea. . .

- Find a ship that's going down the eastern side of the continent, around Cape Horn at the southern tip of South America, and north to California.
- Decide if you're fit enough for the trip – it's over 13,000 miles!

For	*Against*
• No walking.	• Costly.
	• Uncomfortable, dangerous.
	• Dreary journey of 6–12 months.
	• Cramped conditions – passengers packed in tightly.

	• Stale, bad water. • Seasickness (you and the man squashed in beside you). • Wild, treacherous seas, hurricane-force winds. • Stale, rancid food complete with weevils, bugs and bacteria. • A disease called scurvy. • Other diseases that sweep through the passengers like fleas in a dogs' home.

In 1849, more than 15,000 people took the sea route. Amazingly, it's believed that fewer than 50 of them died on the way. (Most of those died from disease, rather than from drowning in stormy seas.)

Don't you feel seasick just thinking about it?
Mmm. Well, you could always try the sea and land route. . .

• Sail to the Caribbean coast of Panama, the narrow

"waist" of America.

- Travel by dugout canoe – so called because it was dug out of a tree trunk – along a steamy, fever-infested river.
- Although you're going west, the land twists in a rather peculiar way just there, so you actually have to travel east. Don't make a mistake!
- Trek through jungle to the Pacific Ocean.
- Board a ship sailing north to San Francisco.

For	*Against*
• Can be done in 6 weeks.	• Costly.
• Land trek takes only a few days.	• Land trek uncomfortable and dangerous.
• Last 20 miles on muleback.	• Snakes, mosquitoes, crocodiles. (Don't fall out of your canoe!)
	• You could be stranded in Panama with no ship – for weeks.
	• Filthy, undrinkable, bug-ridden swamp and river water.
	• Bandits.
	• Malaria, dysentery and cholera.

6,500 set out on this route in 1849, so it couldn't have been that bad. Of course, not everyone made it. Hundreds died in the jungles.

Blimey, there must have been an easier way?
Of course – by wagon, across land. All 2,000 miles of it. . .

- Leave the civilized East by train.
- Take the steamboat down the Missouri River to Independence or St Joseph. These are jumping-off points, where you can team up with others who'd like to travel in convoy, and start your journey.
- Sort out transport, buy food and other necessities. Off you go, heading west on your journey into the unknown.

For	*Against*
• Cheaper than other routes.	• Takes about 6 months.
• You can travel in convoy, for safety.	• Uncomfortable, dangerous.
• You can take your own supply of water.	• In convoy, you'll be half-blinded and choked by dust kicked up by the leaders.
• Good, fresh water	• Sudden rainstorm could

from rivers and streams (for part of the journey).
- Sunshine and fresh air.
- Wagon shelters you from rain.
- Helpful Native Americans (you call them Indians) will trade goods with you and show you where to find water.

wash your wagon down a gully.
- Risk of sunburn and drought.
- Your water supply will eventually go bad.
- Rivers (sources of fresh water) churned by procession of travellers (with oxen).
- Some Native Americans will steal from you, and cheat you.
- Long, dry, dusty stretches of land.
- You'll stink – water's for drinking, not washing.

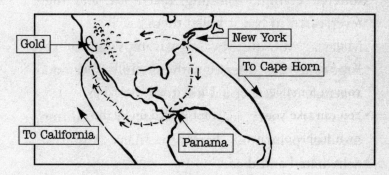

— all sea route   —|—| land and sea route   - - - land route

Are land travellers more likely to make it in one piece?

You'd think so, but many people died on the overland trail. Graves were a common sight along the way – disease being the chief killer. Still, at least you probably won't drown!

What sort of diseases do you mean?

Well, take a look at this lot – and don't forget, the Argonauts had no modern medicines. . .

- Scurvy: caused by lack of fresh veggies and fruit, this disease made the Argonauts' gums swell and bleed, and their teeth fall out. And that's just for starters! If it wasn't treated, they'd bleed inside, and their wounds wouldn't heal.
- Cholera: the result of bad water. The Argonauts suffered cramps, vomiting, diarrhoea, and high fever, often so bad it killed them.
- Malaria: mosquitoes in swamps gave the Argonauts this disease, with its chills, fever and anaemia. Malaria could kill, too.
- Dysentery: very nasty, with fever, vomiting, dreadful pains and diarrhoea. Many Argonauts dehydrated and died.

Not an easy choice, is it?

No. Like thousands of prospectors, though, you've probably got the time, but not the money. You only have about $300 ($6,000 in today's money), but that's enough to kit you out and get you going on the journey by land. There, decision made. You won't be lonely. Between thirty and forty thousand people were heading this way in 1849.

OK, I've emptied the piggy bank – what do I pack?

Spend wisely. If you need it, pack it. If you don't, dump it. Overload your wagon, and you'll find you can't drag it out of mud or a fast-flowing river.

Watch out for the crooks who've suddenly crawled out of the woodwork to make a fast buck by selling you stuff you don't need. Fancy a machine to wash your gold? Don't buy it! Stuff like that ends up tossed over the side of the wagon. You'll find the trail west littered with perfectly good stuff that miners have dumped so they could make it to California:

- rotting food
- broken wheels
- boats
- iron stoves

- the remains of dead fellow travellers
- the bones of dead animals
- empty barrels

Don't make the same mistakes!

FAST FACTS

Gold prospectors had plenty of advice – perhaps too much. Some ads offered essential supplies: guns, medicines, tents, blankets, food and, of course, clothes. But many city people had no idea how rough life was going to get. And advertisers also offered tempting, but useless items, such as an amazing ointment to rub over your body before rolling down the hillside. The idea was that when you got to the bottom, you'd be plastered with gold. If only!

How's about some wheels?

Yep, you'll need a wagon or cart for your family and possessions. And something to pull it. No four-wheel drive here – only four-legged friends.

You mean horses?

Or mules, or even oxen – at least they'd make a good meal if you were starving.

And I'll have to eat, won't I?

Too right! As well as pots, pans, tin plates, cups, cutlery, buckets and bowls, you'll need food. Here's one suggestion for what you should pack:

- 200lb* flour
- 10lb salt
- 10lb coffee
- 20lb sugar
- rice, dried beans and fruit

- baking soda
- vinegar
- 150lbs cured bacon
- cooking fat
- medicines (and whisky)

Oh, and don't forget the water!

No chips then?

Well . . . chips of a sort. You'll cook on an open fire, and for part of your journey there'll be plenty of wood to burn. When there isn't, use buffalo chips.

* 1lb is just over 0.05kg.

Covered wagon

Bow – wooden arch to support cover

Cotton/canvas cover keeps out sun, wind, rain and snow

Tools kept handy for emergencies

Water barrel

Chickens (for eggs and meat)

Wheels – wooden with iron tyre

Buffalo chips?

That's poo to you, and it makes a pretty good blaze.

What about a toolkit?

Think of any and every emergency. Pack guns, knives, farm and carpentry tools, axes and horseshoes.

Right, you have supplies, a wagon, animals to pull it, and a cow or two for milk. Off you go.

Wait a minute, where am I going?

Oh, just follow the wagon in front.

But what if there isn't one?

No problem! There are plenty of maps and guidebooks. You can pick one up easily.

Hang on. How do I know I can trust them?

Good question. Some are written by people with trail experience. Others are rough! They are cobbled together with no thought of danger they might cause.

Use your common sense. Listen to others. Take care, not stupid risks. Then, if disease doesn't get you, and your wagon doesn't crash into a ravine, and you don't starve to death or die of thirst in the desert, well – you're going for gold!

There's gold in them thar hills!

Most of California's new immigrants had come for one reason only. GOLD. And once they got there, their dream was to find the Mother Lode.

Whose mother was she?
Mother Lode was a what, not a who. Gold is found in rocks, and sometimes a large amount forms a vein, or lode. When the rocks are eroded, or worn away, the veins crack and break up, then water picks up broken and crumbled bits and together they flow down hillsides into streams and rivers. The lighter material gets washed on further, but gold settles among the gravel beds of streams. The miners' dream was to find that original vein – the Mother Lode.

Did they dig just any-old-where?
Not if they valued their lives. If a man was going to

mine a piece of land, and wanted to call the gold his own, he had to stake a claim. If he didn't, his gold was up for grabs. Staking a claim was simple. He chose a piece of land, hammered in wooden stakes at the four corners and stuck up a notice saying something like, "I, the undersigned, claim this piece of land for the purpose of mining." Before going off to the local claim officer to make everything legal, he left a tool or two, perhaps a pickaxe, on the land.

Wasn't that asking for trouble?

In the early days, it was the tradition to leave tools on the site while staking a claim. If he had any sense he'd leave someone to guard his claim, otherwise he might come back and find his tools *and* notice gone. Then he'd be the victim of a claim-jumper.

Sounds like some sort of sweatshirt?

No, claim-jumping was outright theft – taking over a man's claimed land after he'd discovered gold – and a new law was quickly brought in to deal with that.

What did the gold look like?

Some of the gold was in the form of dust, finer than the glitter we use on greetings cards. Some looked like flakes. The more exciting stuff was from about the size of a large seed right up to a solid gold nugget.

FAST FACTS

Prospectors in California found almost $2,000,000,000 (that's two billion dollars) in gold dust, flakes and nuggets before the area was all mined out. (A billion in the US means a thousand million, but in the UK it's a million million.)

How did they get it out?

The first prospectors had the easiest job. They picked the gold out of the shallow stream beds. If it was wedged into the ground, they dug it out with a knife.

The visible gold – the "easy pickings" – was gone before the end of 1849. From then on, the miners had to dig a little deeper, and put more effort into their work.

FAST FACTS

After the easy pickings came "pay dirt". This was the gold that was just beneath the surface, covered by a layer of sand or gravel.

Out came the hi-tech equipment, then?

You'd probably call it low-tech. They used a pan. Panning was the simplest way of separating gold from the earth.

The miner scooped up dirt and water from the stream bed, then swirled it round and round, so that the dirt and sand were washed away, leaving the heavier gold at the bottom. At least, that was the idea. If there wasn't any gold there in the first place, it was a waste of time and effort.

FAST FACTS

The pan may have been a very basic piece of equipment, but its simplicity made it the miner's best friend. Not only could he use it to find gold, he could wash his socks in it, and even use it to cook his breakfast!

That sounds nice and easy?

Say that again after you've stood bent over all day in icy water. Those streams the miners worked in flowed from snowy mountain tops. Brrr!

Didn't some brainbox invent a machine?

You *could* call them machines, but they were really simple contraptions made out of wood and nails. One was the cradle, or rocker, which could be worked very efficiently by a pair of miners:

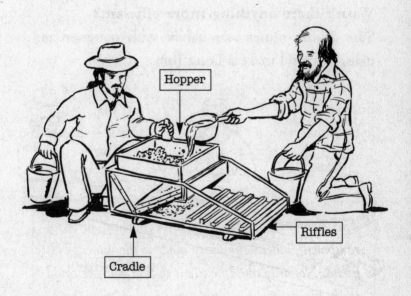

All the lighter rubbish was washed out, leaving the heavier gold caught behind wooden bars called riffles. At least that's what they hoped! Two hundred bucketfuls was a good day's work.

They didn't push themselves then?

Don't you believe it. Between bucketfuls, the bigger stones in the hopper had to be cleaned out ready for the next lot (they didn't want to wash the same ones twice). That's a lot of stones to shift.

Wasn't there anything more efficient?

Sure. If the miner was handy with hammer and nails, he could make a Long Tom:

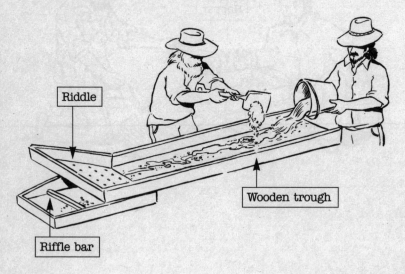

Riddle

Wooden trough

Riffle bar

The gravel was shooshed with water along the trough to the riddle, where the bigger stones were held back and the smaller stuff dropped through the holes into a wooden tray below. Just like the cradle, this tray was fitted with riffle bars to catch the gold . . . If only.

Was that as good as it got?

Nope. It got better. Along came the sluice:

Water flows through constantly – and washes the dirt through.

Longer than the Long Tom

Any gold should be trapped behind bars

More riffle bars

Like the Long Tom, the sluice needed teamwork to operate it. Where there was a team, there were more people to share the gold, but the sluice could sieve a much bigger load per day than the other methods.

That must have made it a doddle?
Hardly, unless a doddle means working from sunrise to sunset in wet or muddy conditions, with aching muscles. And the prospector working on his own still had to light a fire and cook his meal.

What happened when the easy pickings were gone?

Once the surface gold had been mined out, which had happened by about 1852, the average prospector moved on. Deep mining was expensive and difficult, and this is where the big boys came in. Mining companies brought in heavy machinery and explosives, and employed miners who were willing to work in very hazardous conditions. They risked being crushed under falling rock or being blown sky-high.

Was it worth it?

Plenty of people thought so. An ounce of gold (28g) earned its finder $16 and, early on in the Gold Rush, most prospectors could find an average of an ounce each day. But they'd need anything from $8 to $16 a day just for living and working – so they didn't have much left over to send home. Crooked storekeepers made their own pots of gold by keeping prices as high as they could. When you're paying up to $3 for one egg you've got to work pretty hard to earn enough for an omelette. And working hard builds up an appetite. . .

What did they do with the gold when they'd got it?

Any gold that was left over after paying for food, tools, drinking and gambling could be sent to the family back home. After all, that was what most men had come out west for. Adams and Company's Express in San Francisco would transfer money to their offices back east where the miners' families could claim the cash.

FAST FACTS

"How much can you raise in a pinch?" is a saying that dates from the Gold Rush. Store owners would sell goods for a pinch of gold dust, instead of cash. The richest storekeepers were probably the ones with the fattest fingers!

Has all the gold gone now?

No, there's still gold there, but it's deep down and hard to get at, and goldmining's not exactly big business now. However, you can still go on gold-panning holidays and tours of gold country. You won't find much gold, but the tour companies can still make a small fortune!

Bettin', boozin' and law-breakin'!

By the end of 1848 there were getting on for 10,000 gold-miners in California. Within a year there were around 80,000, with more on the way.

FAST FACTS

It's estimated that by 1853, a quarter of a million prospectors were trying their luck in the gold fields.

They all needed somewhere to live. California's climate is warm and sunny – on the whole – and there was bags of room, so the forty-niners weren't too worried about housing.

What's a forty-niner?
All the miners who came prospecting for gold in 1849 were known as forty-niners. Those who came early in the year must have been pretty depressed to

find they were in for a wet spring. They arrived to squalid, muddy conditions. Those who had tents pitched them alongside others, and large camps grew up. These developed into small towns – shanty towns, full of shacks, huts and tents, often with a local store. The mud was uncomfortable, but when summer came, the dust was horrible too, and places like Dry Diggins lived up to their names!

And what's Dry Diggins?

Dry Diggins was a town that grew up round a miners' campsite and the dried-up river bed where they dug. Any area where miners lived together soon got its own name, often based on the character of the place. Dry Diggins later changed its name to Hangtown – you can probably guess why. Rough and Ready, Gold Run and Grizzly Flat are all old mining towns that became so well-established that they're still known by their Gold Rush names today.

What did the women do while their men were mining?

Not much in the way of embroidery and coffee-mornings, that's for sure! Any woman who followed her man across thousands of miles of unknown territory had to be strong and brave. They were resourceful, too. There are tales of women who, busy baking bread or an apple pie, would be approached by a stranger hungrily sniffing the air. The stranger would offer a few dollars for the pie and suddenly the woman would know how to make her own little pot of gold. At a time when domestic work was women's business, they had skills to offer that gold miners were willing – and able – to pay for. They could wash, sew and, above all, cook.

Suppose you wanted to eat out?

You could! The very first cafeteria – a quick-service eatery – appeared in San Francisco during the Gold Rush. And one group of people quickly found their own particular "gold mine" this way – the Chinese. Their restaurants were wildly successful because they worked hard and had good business sense. Chinese meals (eat in or takeaway) were as popular then as they are now.

So it wasn't all work and no play?

Definitely not. Hard-working miners liked a good time when they relaxed. Many were young and most were single (or far from their families). They had energy to burn, even after a hard week's work. Dancing was one way to burn off that energy. A miner would play his fiddle or mouth organ, and the men would dance – sometimes with each other. In those days men always led when a couple danced, so half the miners would tie a ribbon round one arm – which meant they were the "women" and had to follow their partners' steps!

And every town must have had a bar, surely?

You bet! The saloon bar, along with the local store, was one of the first businesses to spring up, and many towns became known by the names of their bars. There was Poverty Bar, Rich Bar, Drunkards Bar, and the not-very-inviting Murderers Bar.

So they must have had some fun?

You could call it fun! Boozing and betting were the chief forms of entertainment. Men who made a pile of money from mining gold all week might lose the lot on Sunday over a game of cards or a horse-race. Tempers ran high and drunken fights were a regular part of the scene, and not just with fists – rifles, shotguns and pistols were always firing off too.

So a nice trip to the theatre was out of the question?

Not entirely. Actors, singers and dancers made their way to Sutter's Fort, now known as Sacramento, and female performers were especially welcome. But the first theatre was virtually a tent, set up beneath a tin roof. Under the hot sun, and with an audience of smelly, unwashed miners, it was known as the "Stinking Tent". There was always the circus, though. The first one rolled up in 1849 and was so popular that within a year miners could choose from two or three.

Gambling, guns, boozing – wasn't that a recipe for trouble?

Yup. With so many people living close together in horrible conditions, each desperate to make his fortune, it would have been a miracle if crime *hadn't* been a problem. Basic laws were essential. The trouble was, there weren't any. At the beginning of the rush, there wasn't much crime. All the prospectors were in the same boat, so they tended to pull together. But as more people packed the diggings, more fortunes were won, lost or stolen, and miners who'd been cheated out of their gold would take desperate measures to get it back.

How desperate is desperate?

Thieving, robbery, assault, stabbings, shootings, murder – these were the sort of crimes committed by those who'd been cheated, or *felt* they'd been cheated, or who'd got too drunk to think straight, or who had no luck in the gold fields . . . or just wanted enough money to get back home.

So the criminals got off scot-free?

There may not have been any official laws, but that didn't stop people using their own brand of justice.

And when they did, revenge was swift. Instant punishments included whipping, banishment, death – or a combination of all three. A group of miners, not necessarily sober, would gather together to decide the fate of the accused man. There was no judge other than "Judge Lynch".

FAST FACTS

Judge Lynch wasn't a real judge at all. The act of hanging a man without a legal trial was – and still is – known as "lynching", after an American called Charles Lynch. He'd taken matters into his own hands during the American Revolution and formed his own court in which judgement and punishment were swift.

Once the verdict was agreed, the punishment was carried out immediately. Most mining towns had their own "hanging tree".

A hanging tree?
Quite literally a tree that was used to hang people from. When things really began to get out of hand, some camps and towns set up vigilante groups.

What's a vigilante when he's at home?

Vigilantes were groups of men who formed a committee to make sure everyone kept the local laws, and to punish them if they didn't. With thousands of new prospectors arriving each week, it became almost impossible to keep peace in San Francisco port. So 103 respectable citizens formed a Committee of Vigilance and put good old Sam Brannan in charge. (Remember Sam? The one who started it all with his bottle of gold dust.) He didn't waste time. Within 24 hours, the vigilantes' first victim was swinging from the end of a noose.

Life was hard, then?

Many prospectors died young: some from disease or mining accidents, others were murdered. Life *was* hard in the gold fields, and it could be very short.

Carry on, California!

By 1853, when the easier pickings had gone, many miners barely made enough to live on, and gave up. They went home sadder and wiser perhaps, but not richer. Others couldn't afford to get back home, and stayed, getting work where they could find it. Although mining continued for about another ten years, the real rush was just about over.

Didn't anybody get rich quick?

Oh, yes. There are many tales of extraordinary single finds, like the $5,000 worth of gold that lay under a tree stump, and the three kilogram nugget a small girl took home to her mum. Reports were made of one miner scooping $20,000 worth of gold pieces in six weeks, and of a young lad who grubbed up over $2,500 worth in a couple of days. Two brothers, who were among the early arrivals at the gold fields, had cleaned up one and a half million dollars in gold by the beginning of 1849!

What did people do with all their lovely lolly?

First of all, you had to make a fortune and, what's more important, hold on to it! John Bidwell, a former guide to immigrants crossing America, made a huge strike. He mined it quickly and used his fortune to buy land – lots of land. He turned to politics and became a Congressman and candidate for President.

William Downie's diggings became so famous for rich pickings that a large camp, called Downieville, soon sprang up around him. He was a generous chap, and spent his money almost as fast as he dug it. After moving on to other goldmining areas, he finally settled down. From sifting gravel to find gold, he ended up making a lot of money selling gravel – without the gold!

Some prospectors returned home in triumph, but some brought their families to California – the Golden State – where they settled and lived comfortably ever after.

Was that as good as it got?
As a matter of fact, no. The real winners in the race to make a fortune did it without digging so much as a teaspoon of Californian soil. They mined their gold from the pockets of the miners themselves!

Who were these people?
Well, here's a few of them. . .

- The shopkeeper
  If wily Sam Brannan planned to sell hammers, he bought up every hammer he could find. Then he could charge whatever price he liked. A prospector, desperate for a hammer to smash open gold-bearing rocks or build a shelter, would have no choice but to pay Sam's price.

FAST FACTS

Sam Brannan became so rich that he was said at one time to own about 20 per cent of San Francisco!

- The tailor
  A 20-year-old German, Levi Strauss, arrived in San Francisco in 1850, planning to sell tent canvas. But most people who needed a tent

already had one. Clever Levi noticed that miners' trousers were often in tatters. With all that rough living, clothes didn't last long. Levi used his canvas to make hard-wearing trousers, and made plenty of money into the bargain. When he ran out of canvas, he bought new fabric called "serge de Nîmes" from Nîmes, in France. He dyed it blue and made trousers that would shrink to fit if you wore them in the bath! Soon "de Nîmes" became "denim". And when Levi added copper rivets, he'd created the Levis you know today.

- The dentist
Once medical student Gardner Colton discovered that nitrous oxide, or laughing gas, was a brilliant anaesthetic, he became a dentist. He went to the gold fields and pulled out thousands of rotten teeth painlessly, but at a price.

FAST FACTS

Gardner Colton, who dropped out of medical school, used to stage hilarious demonstrations of the effects of laughing gas. The story goes that a young shop assistant called Cooley fell about laughing – literally – and injured his leg. When he didn't seem to feel any

---

> *pain, it suddenly dawned on Colton and a dentist*
> *called Wells that they could use the gas for pain-free*
> *dental treatment.*

• The couriers

In 1850, three men began the American Express company. Within a couple of years, two of them – Henry Wells and William Fargo – decided there was business to be made in the Californian gold fields. They started Wells Fargo (good name), with a network of routes to the important mining towns. Wells Fargo had a fleet of top-notch stagecoaches guarded by men with shotguns, and they would buy and sell your gold, or transport it back home. They'd also carry money and mail. In fact, whatever the miners entrusted to reliable, honest Wells Fargo was safely delivered. You could even send for your granny, and they'd deliver her safely!

• The wheelbarrow maker

John Studebaker worked hard making wheelbarrows for miners. He kept out of the saloons and saved every cent he could for almost six years. Then he went home to Indiana to invest his cash in the family wagon-building business. As California grew, so did the wagon business. Eventually the company turned to making cars and became famous for the great Studebaker automobiles.

No doubt there were plenty of losers?
Certainly were. Chief loser had to be John Sutter. The man who triggered the whole Gold Rush died stony broke. Once his staff joined the rush to mine gold, his property was left unprotected. Prospectors overran his land, staking claims, setting up home, mining, and even eating his livestock. His business failed. Everything went wrong for him and, as a last resort, he begged the government for compensation. After all, his loss was California's gain. But by the time the government paid out, it was too late. Sutter was dead.

But James Marshall must have deserved better after spotting the first grains of gold?
It's another sad story. The sawmill went broke and closed down. Superstitious miners believed Marshall had a spooky ability to spot gold, and dogged his footsteps, sometimes turning nasty when he failed to

come up with the goods. Marshall died in 1885, in poverty.

Isn't this all too tragic?

Yes, but things were much worse for the Native Americans. They found their peaceful California homelands overrun by thousands of fortune-hunters. Their crops, and the grass that fed their own animals, were polished off by all the extra horses, oxen and mules the invaders brought with them. The buffalo they hunted for food either moved away or were killed and eaten by the newcomers. Worst of all, new diseases arrived with the prospectors, killing thousands. Before the 1849 Gold Rush there were over 150,000 Native Americans in California. Within 20 years there were fewer than 30,000 left. That really was a tragedy.

FAST FACTS

A colony of sea birds, the common murres, narrowly escaped being wiped out by gold miners. How? The birds, living quietly on rocky islands a few miles from San Francisco, provided a constant supply of eggs for hungry Californians. Millions were taken, sold and eaten, and the murre colony is still recovering today.

And what sort of state was California left in?

It wasn't *in* a state – it *became* a state. In 1850, the government announced that the area known as California was to join the other 30 United States of America.

By then the population of California had rocketed to over 100,000. Where towns had sprung up, shops, manufacturing industries, stagecoach depots and railway stations soon appeared. Masses of money was invested in the area – not just for mining, but for other industries, such as ship-building. The little port of San Francisco, almost empty when people rushed inland to the gold diggings, blossomed into a great financial centre because of all the new business. Wherever people lived, doctors, dentists, teachers and lawyers settled, too. And so did the Chinese, into the area that became known as San Francisco's Chinatown.

And Sutter's Fort?

That became the city of Sacramento, now California's capital!

So the Gold Rush was a good thing?

On the whole, yes. Although gold made only a few people hugely wealthy, the Gold Rush brought prosperity to California. The forty-niners prepared the way for thousands of settlers. People migrating to California from the east coast, and from all round the world, found a fairly well-established community waiting for them.

California now has a population of more than 30 million.

So what did the gold rush mean to America?
1849 was a turning-point in the history of America. The gap between the west and east coasts had been bridged and success for the Golden State of California was assured.

Were there other gold rushes?
Yes. In fact, Australia's rush happened soon after California's, in 1851. Again, a chance discovery sparked it off. It was slightly different from the American experience, though. California's gold was mainly dust or small flakes and grains, but Australia had BIG nuggets – up to 90 kg!

South Africa was next, when a miner at the famous Kimberley diamond mines found gold on farm land. Big mining companies moved in and the gold industry grew and grew.

The one that's best known, however, is the Klondike gold rush in the Yukon, Canada, right at the end of the nineteenth century. It only lasted a few years, but it turned the trading post of Dawson into a full-to-bursting boom town for a while. When silent-film star Charlie Chaplin made his film, *The Gold Rush,* set in the Klondike, it became really famous.

All these rushes meant people moving to new areas, whether it was to work for a big company, or to go it alone.

Could it happen again?
Possibly. Gold's still being mined from the earth. Maybe someday, somewhere, someone else will bend over to examine a funny-looking pebble, and will straighten up with a cry of, "Gold! *Gold!* GOLD!"

Further Information

Internet addresses:

If you'd like to know more, why not visit these websites?

http://www.museumca.org/goldrush
For a virtual tour of the gold rush exhibition at the Oakland Museum of California.

http://www.pbs.org/goldrush/funfacts.html
For weird and wonderful stories about the Californian goldrush.

SPEEDY READS

Want to find out the facts, and quick?
Make a mad dash to get some other speedy reads!

Moon Landing
by Nick Arnold
Moon Landing tells the true story and answers
the questions on the most important event in
scientific history.

The True Mystery of the Mary Celeste
by Rachel Wright
The True Mystery of the Mary Celeste answers
all your vital questions on the greatest sea
mystery ever.

Titanic
by Alan MacDonald
Titanic tells the true story and answers all your
questions on the biggest sea disaster of the
20th century.

**Speedy Reads – no more than you need
to know!**

TOP·TEN

Dickens Stories
by Valerie Wilding

What was top of the pops in Victorian times? Want to know which Dickens story's had the number one slot since the 19th century? It could be…

Great Expectations – take a peep in Pip's diary and expect takes of escaped convicts and romance gone horribly wrong!

A Tale of Two Cities – The French are revolting and anyone could end up on the gory guillotine. Can our heroes and heroines keep their heads?

Oliver Twist – Starved orphan kidnapped by bad Bill Sikes! Join the manhunt with the Crimes R Us TV crew.

WITH top ten fact sections, including crime, punishment, nasty nightmare schools and kids up chimneys.

Dickens stories as you've never seen them before.

TOP·TEN

Classics
by Valerie Wilding

What are the greatest stories of all time?
Want to know which classic story has the
number one slot out of hundreds of terrific tales?
It could be…

Around the World in Eighty Days – Quick!
Join the chase as Detective Fix follows Phileas
Fogg and Passepartout to the ends of the earth
and back again.
Black Beauty – come along for the ride of
your life through fires and floods and get the
story straight from the horse's mouth.
Wuthering Heights – Mystery and romance on
the moors with Heathcliff and Cathy – it's wild!
With top ten fact sections, including outrageous
explorers' tales, a travel quide for fantasy islands,
and ten real cut-throat pirates!

**Classic stories as you've never seen
them before.**

Dreadful Drama
by Rachel Wright

First ancient Greek guys put on masks and
acted out top tales.
Next Shakespeare and his pals had some huge hits.
Now the world's a stage to all sorts – from plays
with no words to actors with no clothes!

In this behind the scenes guide you'll meet an
actress who slept in a coffin, a playwright who
lost the plot, and a director with all the talent of
a corridor. You'll turn the spotlight on stage
fights, fake props and special effects, and find out
if you've got what it takes to write a smash-hit
play or be a mega stage star.

So lights down for some dreadfully dramatic
action. It's quite a performance.

**If you want to be in the know, get
The Knowledge!**